FORWARD/COMMENTARY

The National Institute of Standards and Technology (NIST) is a measurement standards laboratory, and a non-regulatory agency of the United States Department of Commerce. Its mission is to promote innovation and industrial competitiveness. Founded in 1901, as the National Bureau of Standards, NIST was formed with the mandate to provide standard weights and measures, and to serve as the national physical laboratory for the United States. With a world-class measurement and testing laboratory encompassing a wide range of areas of computer science, mathematics, statistics, and systems engineering, NIST's cybersecurity program supports its overall mission to promote U.S. innovation and industrial competitiveness by advancing measurement science, standards, and related technology through research and development in ways that enhance economic security and improve our quality of life.

The need for cybersecurity standards and best practices that address interoperability, usability and privacy has been shown to be critical for the nation. NIST's cybersecurity programs seek to enable greater development and application of practical, innovative security technologies and methodologies that enhance the country's ability to address current and future computer and information security challenges.

The cybersecurity publications produced by NIST cover a wide range of cybersecurity concepts that are carefully designed to work together to produce a holistic approach to cybersecurity primarily for government agencies and constitute the best practices used by industry. This holistic strategy to cybersecurity covers the gamut of security subjects from development of secure encryption standards for communication and storage of information while at rest, to how best to recover from a cyber-attack.

Why buy a book you can download for free? We print these books so you don't have to.

Some books are available only in electronic media and you need a hard copy. So, you have to print it yourself – not always easy when you share a LAN printer with 100 other people.

We at 4th Watch Books are former government employees, so we know how people actually use these standards. When a new standard is released, an engineer prints it out, punches holes and puts it in a 3-ring binder. While this is not a big deal for a 5 or 10-page document, many work documents are over 100 pages and printing a large document is a time-consuming effort. An engineer that's paid $75 an hour could spend hours simply printing out the tools needed to do the job. That's time that could be better spent doing engineering. We publish these documents so engineers can focus on what they were hired to do – engineering. It's much more cost-effective to simply order the latest version from Amazon.com. If you like the service we provide, please leave positive review on Amazon so we can continue to print books you need. If there is a standard you would like to see printed, let us know. Our web site is Cybah.webplus.net

See a list of all the docs we print on our CyberSecurity Standards Library™ DVD.

NIST

National Institute of
Standards and Technology
U.S. Department of Commerce

Special Publication 800-41
Revision 1

Guidelines on Firewalls and Firewall Policy

Recommendations of the National Institute of Standards and Technology

Karen Scarfone
Paul Hoffman

NIST Special Publication 800-41 Revision 1

Guidelines on Firewalls and Firewall Policy

Recommendations of the National Institute of Standards and Technology

Karen Scarfone
Paul Hoffman

COMPUTER SECURITY

Computer Security Division
Information Technology Laboratory
National Institute of Standards and Technology
Gaithersburg, MD 20899-8930

September 2009

U.S. Department of Commerce

Gary Locke, Secretary

National Institute of Standards and Technology

Patrick D. Gallagher, Deputy Director

Reports on Computer Systems Technology

The Information Technology Laboratory (ITL) at the National Institute of Standards and Technology (NIST) promotes the U.S. economy and public welfare by providing technical leadership for the nation's measurement and standards infrastructure. ITL develops tests, test methods, reference data, proof of concept implementations, and technical analysis to advance the development and productive use of information technology. ITL's responsibilities include the development of technical, physical, administrative, and management standards and guidelines for the cost-effective security and privacy of sensitive unclassified information in Federal computer systems. This Special Publication 800-series reports on ITL's research, guidance, and outreach efforts in computer security and its collaborative activities with industry, government, and academic organizations.

National Institute of Standards and Technology Special Publication 800-41 Revision 1
Natl. Inst. Stand. Technol. Spec. Publ. 800-41 rev1, 48 pages (Sep. 2009)

Acknowledgments

The authors, Karen Scarfone of the National Institute of Standards and Technology (NIST) and Paul Hoffman of the Virtual Private Network Consortium, wish to thank their colleagues who reviewed drafts of this document and contributed to its technical content. The authors would like to acknowledge Tim Grance, Murugiah Souppaya, Sheila Frankel, and Gale Richter of NIST, and Matthew Goche, David Klug, Logan Lodge, John Pearce, Noel Richards, Anne Roudabush, and Steven Sharma of Booz Allen Hamilton, for their keen and insightful assistance throughout the development of the document. Special thanks go to Brahim Asfahani of Booz Allen Hamilton for his contributions to early drafts of the document. The authors also thank all the reviewers who provided feedback during the public comment period, particularly Joel Snyder (Opus One), Ron Colvin (National Aeronautics and Space Administration [NASA]), Dean Farrington (Wells Fargo), Raffael Marty (Splunk), and David Newman (Network Test).

The authors also wish to express their thanks to the individuals and organizations that contributed to the original version of the publication, including John Wack of NIST and Ken Cutler and Jamie Pole of the MIS Training Institute, who authored the original version, and other contributors and reviewers—particularly Peter Batista and Wayne Bavry (U.S. Treasury); Harriet Feldman (Integrated Computer Engineering, Inc.); Rex Sanders (U.S. Geological Survey); and Timothy Grance, D. Richard Kuhn, Peter Mell, Gale Richter, and Murugiah Souppaya (NIST).

Table of Contents

List of Appendices

List of Figures

List of Tables

Executive Summary

Firewalls are devices or programs that control the flow of network traffic between networks or hosts that employ differing security postures. At one time, most firewalls were deployed at network perimeters. This provided some measure of protection for internal hosts, but it could not recognize all instances and forms of attack, and attacks sent from one internal host to another often do not pass through network firewalls. Because of these and other factors, network designers now often include firewall functionality at places other than the network perimeter to provide an additional layer of security, as well as to protect mobile devices that are placed directly onto external networks.

Threats have gradually moved from being most prevalent in lower layers of network traffic to the application layer, which has reduced the general effectiveness of firewalls in stopping threats carried through network communications. However, firewalls are still needed to stop the significant threats that continue to work at lower layers of network traffic. Firewalls can also provide some protection at the application layer, supplementing the capabilities of other network security technologies.

There are several types of firewalls, each with varying capabilities to analyze network traffic and allow or block specific instances by comparing traffic characteristics to existing policies. Understanding the capabilities of each type of firewall, and designing firewall policies and acquiring firewall technologies that effectively address an organization's needs, are critical to achieving protection for network traffic flows. This document provides an overview of firewall technologies and discusses their security capabilities and relative advantages and disadvantages in detail. It also provides examples of where firewalls can be placed within networks, and the implications of deploying firewalls in particular locations. The document also makes recommendations for establishing firewall policies and for selecting, configuring, testing, deploying, and managing firewall solutions.

This document does not cover technologies that are called "firewalls" but primarily examine only application layer activity, not lower layers of network traffic. Technologies that focus on activity for a particular type of application, such as email firewalls that block email messages with suspicious content, are not covered in detail in this document.

To improve the effectiveness and security of their firewalls, organizations should implement the following recommendations:

Create a firewall policy that specifies how firewalls should handle inbound and outbound network traffic.

A firewall policy defines how an organization's firewalls should handle inbound and outbound network traffic for specific IP addresses and address ranges, protocols, applications, and content types based on the organization's information security policies. Organizations should conduct risk analysis to develop a list of the types of traffic needed by the organization and how they must be secured—including which types of traffic can traverse a firewall under what circumstances. Examples of policy requirements include permitting only necessary Internet Protocol (IP) protocols to pass, appropriate source and destination IP addresses to be used, particular Transmission Control Protocol (TCP) and User Datagram Protocol (UDP) ports to be accessed, and certain Internet Control Message Protocol (ICMP) types and codes to be used. Generally, all inbound and outbound traffic not expressly permitted by the firewall policy should be blocked because such traffic is not needed by the organization. This practice reduces the risk of attack and can also decrease the volume of traffic carried on the organization's networks.

Identify all requirements that should be considered when determining which firewall to implement.

There are many considerations that organizations should include in their firewall selection and planning processes. Organizations need to determine which network areas need to be protected, and which types of firewall technologies will be most effective for the types of traffic that require protection. Several important performance considerations also exist, as well as concerns regarding the integration of the firewall into existing network and security infrastructures. Additionally, firewall solution design involves requirements relating to physical environment and personnel as well as consideration of possible future needs, such as plans to adopt new IPv6 technologies or virtual private networks (VPN).

Create rulesets that implement the organization's firewall policy while supporting firewall performance.

Firewall rulesets should be as specific as possible with regards to the network traffic they control. To create a ruleset involves determining what types of traffic are required, including protocols the firewall may need to use for management purposes. The details of creating rulesets vary widely by type of firewall and specific products, but many firewalls can have their performance improved by optimizing firewall rulesets. For example, some firewalls check traffic against rules in a sequential manner until a match is found; for these firewalls, rules that have the highest chance of matching traffic patterns should be placed at the top of the list wherever possible.

Manage firewall architectures, policies, software, and other components throughout the life of the firewall solutions.

There are many aspects to firewall management. For example, choosing the type or types of firewalls to deploy and their positions within the network can significantly affect the security policies that the firewalls can enforce. Policy rules may need to be updated as the organization's requirements change, such as when new applications or hosts are implemented within the network. Firewall component performance also needs to be monitored to enable potential resource issues to be identified and addressed before components become overwhelmed. Logs and alerts should also be continuously monitored to identify threats—both successful and unsuccessful. Firewall rulesets and policies should be managed by a formal change management control process because of their potential to impact security and business operations, with ruleset reviews or tests performed periodically to ensure continued compliance with the organization's policies. Firewall software should be patched as vendors provide updates to address vulnerabilities.

1. Introduction

1.1 Authority

The National Institute of Standards and Technology (NIST) developed this document in furtherance of its statutory responsibilities under the Federal Information Security Management Act (FISMA) of 2002, Public Law 107-347.

NIST is responsible for developing standards and guidelines, including minimum requirements, for providing adequate information security for all agency operations and assets; but such standards and guidelines shall not apply to national security systems. This guideline is consistent with the requirements of the Office of Management and Budget (OMB) Circular A-130, Section 8b(3), "Securing Agency Information Systems," as analyzed in A-130, Appendix IV: Analysis of Key Sections. Supplemental information is provided in A-130, Appendix III.

This guideline has been prepared for use by Federal agencies. It may be used by nongovernmental organizations on a voluntary basis and is not subject to copyright, though attribution is desired.

Nothing in this document should be taken to contradict standards and guidelines made mandatory and binding on Federal agencies by the Secretary of Commerce under statutory authority, nor should these guidelines be interpreted as altering or superseding the existing authorities of the Secretary of Commerce, Director of the OMB, or any other Federal official.

1.2 Purpose and Scope

This document seeks to assist organizations in understanding the capabilities of firewall technologies and firewall policies. It provides practical guidance on developing firewall policies and selecting, configuring, testing, deploying, and managing firewalls.

1.3 Audience

This document has been created primarily for technical information technology (IT) personnel such as network, security, and system engineers and administrators who are responsible for firewall design, selection, deployment, and management. Other IT personnel with network and system security responsibilities may also find this document to be useful. The content assumes some basic knowledge of networking and network security.

1.4 Document Structure

The remainder of this document is organized into four major sections:

■   Section 2 provides an overview of a number of network firewall technologies—including packet filtering, stateful inspection, and application-proxy gatewaying—and also provides information on host-based and personal firewalls.

■   Section 3 discusses the placement of firewalls within network architectures.

■   Section 4 discusses firewall policies and makes recommendations on the types of traffic that should be specified as prohibited.

■ Section 5 provides an overview of firewall planning and implementation. It lists factors to consider when selecting firewall solutions, and provides recommendations for firewall configuration, testing, deployment, and management.

The document also contains appendices with supporting material:

■ Appendices A and B contain a glossary and an acronym and abbreviation list, respectively.

■ Appendix C lists print and online resources that may be of use in gaining a better understanding of firewalls.

2. Overview of Firewall Technologies

Firewalls are devices or programs that control the flow of network traffic between networks or hosts that employ differing security postures. While firewalls are often discussed in the context of Internet connectivity, they may also have applicability in other network environments. For example, many enterprise networks employ firewalls to restrict connectivity to and from the internal networks used to service more sensitive functions, such as accounting or personnel. By employing firewalls to control connectivity to these areas, an organization can prevent unauthorized access to its systems and resources. Inclusion of a proper firewall provides an additional layer of security. Organizations often need to use firewalls to meet security requirements from mandates (e.g., FISMA); some mandates, such as the Payment Card Industry (PCI) Data Security Standard,[1] specifically require firewalling.

Several types of firewall technologies are available. One way of comparing their capabilities is to look at the Transmission Control Protocol/Internet Protocol (TCP/IP) layers that each is able to examine. TCP/IP communications are composed of four layers that work together to transfer data between hosts. When a user wants to transfer data across networks, the data is passed from the highest layer through intermediate layers to the lowest layer, with each layer adding more information. The lowest layer sends the accumulated data through the physical network, with the data then passed upwards through the layers to its destination. Simply put, the data produced by a layer is encapsulated in a larger container by the layer below it. The four TCP/IP layers, from highest to lowest, are shown in Figure 2-1.

Application Layer. This layer sends and receives data for particular applications, such as Domain Name System (DNS), Hypertext Transfer Protocol (HTTP), and Simple Mail Transfer Protocol (SMTP). The application layer itself has layers of protocols within it. For example, SMTP encapsulates the Request for Comments (RFC) 2822 message syntax, which encapsulates Multipurpose Internet Mail Extensions (MIME), which can encapsulate other formats such as Hypertext Markup Language (HTML).
Transport Layer. This layer provides connection-oriented or connectionless services for transporting application layer services between networks, and can optionally ensure communications reliability. Transmission Control Protocol (TCP) and User Datagram Protocol (UDP) are commonly used transport layer protocols.[2]
IP Layer (also known as the Network Layer). This layer routes packets across networks. Internet Protocol version 4 (IPv4) is the fundamental network layer protocol for TCP/IP. Other commonly used protocols at the network layer are Internet Protocol version 6 (IPv6), ICMP, and Internet Group Management Protocol (IGMP).
Hardware Layer (also known as the Data Link Layer). This layer handles communications on the physical network components. The best known data link layer protocol is Ethernet.

Figure 2-1. TCP/IP Layers

Addresses at the data link layer, which are assigned to network interfaces, are referred to as *media access control (MAC) addresses*—an example of this is an Ethernet address that belongs to an Ethernet card. Firewall policies rarely concern themselves with the data link layer. Addresses at the network layer are referred to as *IP addresses*. The transport layer identifies specific network applications and communication sessions as opposed to network addresses; a host may have any number of transport layer sessions with other hosts on the same network. The transport layer may also include the notion of *ports*— a destination port number generally identifies a service listening on the destination host, and a source port usually identifies the port number on the source host that the destination host should reply to. Transport protocols such as TCP and UDP have ports, while other transport protocols do not. The combination of

---

[1]   The PCI Data Security Standard may apply to some Federal agencies. It is defined at https://www.pcisecuritystandards.org/.
[2]   The differences between TCP and UDP are explained by several of the print resources listed in Appendix C.

source IP address and port with destination IP address and port helps define the session. The highest layer represents end user applications—firewalls can inspect application traffic and use it as the basis for policy decisions.

Basic firewalls operate on one or a few layers—typically the lower layers—while more advanced firewalls examine all of the layers shown in Figure 2-1. Those that examine more layers can perform more granular and thorough examinations. Firewalls that understand the application layer can potentially accommodate advanced applications and protocols and provide services that are user-oriented. For example, a firewall that only handles lower layers cannot usually identify specific users, but a firewall with application layer capabilities can enforce user authentication and log events to specific users.

2.1 Firewall Technologies

This section of the publication provides an overview of firewall technologies and basic information on the capabilities of several commonly used types. Firewalling is often combined with other technologies—most notably routing—and many technologies often associated with firewalls are more accurately part of these other technologies. For example, network address translation (NAT) is sometimes thought of as a firewall technology, but it is actually a routing technology. Many firewalls also include content filtering features to enforce organization policies not directly related to security. Some firewalls include intrusion prevention system (IPS) technologies, which can react to attacks that they detect to prevent damage to systems protected by the firewall.

Firewalls are often placed at the perimeter of a network. Such a firewall can be said to have an *external* and *internal* interface, with the external interface being the one on the outside of the network. These two interfaces are sometimes referred to as *unprotected* and *protected*, respectively. However, saying that something is or is not protected is often inappropriate because a firewall's policies can work in both directions; for example, there might be a policy to prevent executable code from being sent from inside the perimeter to sites outside the perimeter.

2.1.1 Packet Filtering

The most basic feature of a firewall is the *packet filter*. Older firewalls that were only packet filters were essentially routing devices that provided access control functionality for host addresses and communication sessions. These devices, also known as *stateless inspection firewalls*, do not keep track of the state of each flow of traffic that passes though the firewall; this means, for example, that they cannot associate multiple requests within a single session to each other. Packet filtering is at the core of most modern firewalls, but there are few firewalls sold today that only do stateless packet filtering. Unlike more advanced filters, packet filters are not concerned about the content of packets. Their access control functionality is governed by a set of directives referred to as a *ruleset*. Packet filtering capabilities are built into most operating systems and devices capable of routing; the most common example of a pure packet filtering device is a network router that employs access control lists.

In their most basic form, firewalls with packet filters operate at the network layer. This provides network access control based on several pieces of information contained in a packet, including:

■ The packet's source IP address—the address of the host from which the packet originated (such as 192.168.1.1)

■ The packet's destination address—the address of the host the packet is trying to reach (e.g., 192.168.2.1)

- The network or transport protocol being used to communicate between source and destination hosts, such as TCP, UDP, or ICMP

- Possibly some characteristics of the transport layer communications sessions, such as session source and destination ports (e.g., TCP 80 for the destination port belonging to a web server, TCP 1320 for the source port belonging to a personal computer accessing the server)

- The interface being traversed by the packet, and its direction (inbound or outbound).

Filtering inbound traffic is known as *ingress filtering*. Outgoing traffic can also be filtered, a process referred to as *egress filtering*. Here, organizations can implement restrictions on their internal traffic, such as blocking the use of external file transfer protocol (FTP) servers or preventing denial of service (DoS) attacks from being launched from within the organization against outside entities. Organizations should only permit outbound traffic that uses the source IP addresses in use by the organization—a process that helps block traffic with spoofed addresses from leaking onto other networks. Spoofed addresses can be caused by malicious events such as malware infections or compromised hosts being used to launch attacks, or by inadvertent misconfigurations.

Stateless packet filters are generally vulnerable to attacks and exploits that take advantage of problems within the TCP/IP specification and protocol stack. For example, many packet filters are unable to detect when a packet's network layer addressing information has been spoofed or otherwise altered, or uses options that are permitted by standards but generally used for malicious purposes, such as IP source routing. Spoofing attacks, such as using incorrect addresses in the packet headers, are generally employed by intruders to bypass the security controls implemented in a firewall platform. Firewalls that operate at higher layers can thwart some spoofing attacks by verifying that a session is established, or by authenticating users before allowing traffic to pass. Because of this, most firewalls that use packet filters also maintain some state information for the packets that traverse the firewall.

Some packet filters can specifically filter packets that are fragmented. Packet fragmentation is allowed by the TCP/IP specifications and is encouraged in situations where it is needed. However, packet fragmentation has been used to make some attacks harder to detect (by placing them within fragmented packets), and unusual fragmentation has also been used as a form of attack. For example, some network-based attacks have used packets that should not exist in normal communications, such as sending some fragments of a packet but not the first fragment, or sending packet fragments that overlap each other. To prevent the use of fragmented packets in attacks, some firewalls have been configured to block fragmented packets.

Today, fragmented packets on the Internet often occur not because of attacks, but because of virtual private networking (VPN) technologies that encapsulate packets within other packets. If encapsulating a packet would cause the new packet to exceed the maximum permitted size for the medium it will be transmitted on, the packet must be fragmented. Fragmented packets being blocked by firewalls is a common cause of VPN interoperability issues.

Some firewalls can reassemble fragments before passing them to the inside network, although this requires additional firewall resources, particularly memory. Firewalls that have this reassembly feature must implement it carefully, otherwise someone can readily mount a denial-of-service attack. Choosing whether to block, reassemble, or pass fragmented packets is a tradeoff between overall network interoperability and full system security. Given this, automatic blocking of all fragmented packets is not recommended because of the legitimate and necessary uses of fragmentation on the Internet.

2.1.2 Stateful Inspection

Stateful inspection improves on the functions of packet filters by tracking the state of connections and blocking packets that deviate from the expected state. This is accomplished by incorporating greater awareness of the transport layer. As with packet filtering, stateful inspection intercepts packets at the network layer and inspects them to see if they are permitted by an existing firewall rule, but unlike packet filtering, stateful inspection keeps track of each connection in a state table. While the details of state table entries vary by firewall product, they typically include source IP address, destination IP address, port numbers, and connection state information.

Three major states exist for TCP traffic—connection establishment, usage, and termination (which refers to both an endpoint requesting that a connection be closed and a connection with a long period of inactivity.) Stateful inspection in a firewall examines certain values in the TCP headers to monitor the state of each connection. Each new packet is compared by the firewall to the firewall's state table to determine if the packet's state contradicts its expected state. For example, an attacker could generate a packet with a header indicating it is part of an established connection, in hopes it will pass through a firewall. If the firewall uses stateful inspection, it will first verify that the packet is part of an established connection listed in the state table.

In the simplest case, a firewall will allow through any packet that seems to be part of an open connection (or even a connection that is not yet fully established). However, many firewalls are more cognizant of the state machines for protocols such as TCP and UDP, and they will block packets that do not adhere strictly to the appropriate state machine. For example, it is common for firewalls to check attributes such as TCP sequence numbers and reject packets that are out of sequence. When a firewall provides NAT services, it often includes NAT information in its state table.

Table 2-1 provides an example of a state table. If a device on the internal network (shown here as 192.168.1.100) attempts to connect to a device outside the firewall (192.0.2.71), the connection attempt is first checked to see if it is permitted by the firewall ruleset. If it is permitted, an entry is added to the state table that indicates a new session is being initiated, as shown in the first entry under "Connection State" in Table 2-1. If 192.0.2.71 and 192.168.1.100 complete the three-way TCP handshake, the connection state will change to "established" and all subsequent traffic matching the entry will be allowed to pass through the firewall.

Table 2-1. State Table Example

Source Address	Source Port	Destination Address	Destination Port	Connection State
192.168.1.100	1030	192.0.2.71	80	Initiated
192.168.1.102	1031	10.12.18.74	80	Established
192.168.1.101	1033	10.66.32.122	25	Established
192.168.1.106	1035	10.231.32.12	79	Established

Because some protocols, most notably UDP, are connectionless and do not have a formal process for initializing, establishing, and terminating a connection, their state cannot be established at the transport layer as it is for TCP. For these protocols, most firewalls with stateful inspection are only able to track the source and destination IP addresses and ports. UDP packets must still match an entry in the state table based on source and destination IP address and port information to be permitted to pass—a DNS response from an external source would be permitted to pass only if the firewall had previously seen a corresponding DNS query from an internal source. Since the firewall is unable to determine when a session has ended, the entry is removed from the state table after a preconfigured timeout value is reached. Application-level firewalls that are able to recognize DNS over UDP will terminate a session after a DNS response is received, and may act similarly with the Network Time Protocol (NTP).

2.1.3 Application Firewalls

A newer trend in stateful inspection is the addition of a *stateful protocol analysis* capability, referred to by some vendors as *deep packet inspection*. Stateful protocol analysis improves upon standard stateful inspection by adding basic intrusion detection technology—an inspection engine that analyzes protocols at the application layer to compare vendor-developed profiles of benign protocol activity against observed events to identify deviations. This allows a firewall to allow or deny access based on how an application is running over the network. For instance, an application firewall can determine if an email message contains a type of attachment that the organization does not permit (such as an executable file), or if instant messaging (IM) is being used over port 80 (typically used for HTTP). Another feature is that it can block connections over which specific actions are being performed (e.g., users could be prevented from using the FTP "put" command, which allows users to write files to the FTP server). This feature can also be used to allow or deny web pages that contain particular types of active content, such as Java or ActiveX, or that have SSL certificates signed by a particular certificate authority (CA), such as a compromised or revoked CA.

Application firewalls can enable the identification of unexpected sequences of commands, such as issuing the same command repeatedly or issuing a command that was not preceded by another command on which it is dependent. These suspicious commands often originate from buffer overflow attacks, DoS attacks, malware, and other forms of attack carried out within application protocols such as HTTP. Another common feature is input validation for individual commands, such as minimum and maximum lengths for arguments. For example, a username argument with a length of 1000 characters is suspicious—even more so if it contains binary data. Application firewalls are available for many common protocols including HTTP, database (such as SQL), email (SMTP, Post Office Protocol [POP], and Internet Message Access Protocol [IMAP])[3], voice over IP (VoIP), and Extensible Markup Language (XML).[4]

Another feature found in some application firewalls involves enforcing application state machines, which are essentially checks on the traffic's compliance to the standard for the protocol in question. This compliance checking, sometimes call "RFC compliance" because most protocols are defined in RFCs issued by the Internet Engineering Task Force (IETF), can be a mixed blessing. Many products implement protocols in ways that almost, but not completely, match the specification, so it is usually necessary to let such implementations communicate across the firewall. Compliance checking is only useful when it detects and blocks communication that can be harmful to protected systems.

Firewalls with both stateful inspection and stateful protocol analysis capabilities are not full-fledged intrusion detection and prevention systems (IDPS), which usually offer much more extensive attack detection and prevention capabilities. For example, IDPSs also use signature-based and/or anomaly-based analysis to detect additional problems within network traffic.[5]

---

[3]   For additional information about email security, see NIST Special Publication (SP) 800-45 Version 2, *Guidelines on Electronic Mail Security* (http://csrc.nist.gov/publications/PubsSPs.html).

[4]   For additional information about XML and XML firewalls, see NIST SP 800-95, *Guide to Secure Web Services* (http://csrc.nist.gov/publications/PubsSPs.html).

[5]   For additional information about IDPS, see NIST SP 800-94, *Guide to Intrusion Detection and Prevention Systems (IDPS)* (http://csrc.nist.gov/publications/PubsSPs.html).

2.1.4 Application-Proxy Gateways

An *application-proxy gateway* is a feature of advanced firewalls that combines lower-layer access control with upper-layer functionality. These firewalls contain a proxy agent that acts as an intermediary between two hosts that wish to communicate with each other, and never allows a direct connection between them. Each successful connection attempt actually results in the creation of two separate connections—one between the client and the proxy server, and another between the proxy server and the true destination. The proxy is meant to be transparent to the two hosts—from their perspectives there is a direct connection. Because external hosts only communicate with the proxy agent, internal IP addresses are not visible to the outside world. The proxy agent interfaces directly with the firewall ruleset to determine whether a given instance of network traffic should be allowed to transit the firewall.

In addition to the ruleset, some proxy agents have the ability to require authentication of each individual network user. This authentication can take many forms, including user ID and password, hardware or software token, source address, and biometrics.

Like application firewalls, the proxy gateway operates at the application layer and can inspect the actual content of the traffic. These gateways also perform the TCP handshake with the source system and are able to protect against exploitations at each step of a communication. In addition, gateways can make decisions to permit or deny traffic based on information in the application protocol headers or payloads. Once the gateway determines that data should be permitted, it is forwarded to the destination host.

Application-proxy gateways are quite different than application firewalls. First, an application-proxy gateway can offer a higher level of security for some applications because it prevents direct connections between two hosts and it inspects traffic content to identify policy violations. Another potential advantage is that some application-proxy gateways have the ability to decrypt packets (e.g., SSL-protected payloads), examine them, and re-encrypt them before sending them on to the destination host. Data that the gateway cannot decrypt is passed directly through to the application. When choosing the type of firewall to deploy, it is important to decide whether the firewall actually needs to act as an application proxy so that it can match the specific policies needed by the organization.

Firewalls with application-proxy gateways can also have several disadvantages when compared to packet filtering and stateful inspection. First, because of the "full packet awareness" of application-proxy gateways, the firewall spends much more time reading and interpreting each packet. Because of this, some of these gateways are poorly suited to high-bandwidth or real-time applications—but application-proxy gateways rated for high bandwidth are available. To reduce the load on the firewall, a dedicated proxy server (discussed in Section 2.1.5) can be used to secure less time-sensitive services such as email and most web traffic. Another disadvantage is that application-proxy gateways tend to be limited in terms of support for new network applications and protocols—an individual, application-specific proxy agent is required for each type of network traffic that needs to transit a firewall. Many application-proxy gateway firewall vendors provide generic proxy agents to support undefined network protocols or applications. Those generic agents tend to negate many of the strengths of the application-proxy gateway architecture because they simply allow traffic to "tunnel" through the firewall.

2.1.5 Dedicated Proxy Servers

Dedicated proxy servers differ from application-proxy gateways in that while dedicated proxy servers retain proxy control of traffic, they usually have much more limited firewalling capabilities. They are described in this section because of their close relationship to application-proxy gateway firewalls. Many dedicated proxy servers are application-specific, and some actually perform analysis and validation of common application protocols such as HTTP. Because these servers have limited firewalling capabilities, such as simply blocking traffic based on its source or destination, they are typically deployed behind traditional firewall platforms. Typically, a main firewall could accept inbound traffic, determine which application is being targeted, and hand off traffic to the appropriate proxy server (e.g., email proxy). This server would perform filtering or logging operations on the traffic, then forward it to internal systems. A proxy server could also accept outbound traffic directly from internal systems, filter or log the traffic, and pass it to the firewall for outbound delivery. An example of this is an HTTP proxy deployed behind the firewall—users would need to connect to this proxy en route to connecting to external web servers. Dedicated proxy servers are generally used to decrease firewall workload and conduct specialized filtering and logging that might be difficult to perform on the firewall itself.

In recent years, the use of *inbound* proxy servers has decreased dramatically. This is because an inbound proxy server must mimic the capabilities of the real server it is protecting, which becomes nearly impossible when protecting a server with many features. Using a proxy server with fewer capabilities than the server it is protecting renders the non-matched capabilities unusable. Additionally, the essential features that inbound proxy servers should have (logging, access control, etc.) are usually built into the real servers. Most proxy servers now in use are *outbound* proxy servers, with the most common being HTTP proxies.

Figure 2-2 shows a sample diagram of a network employing a dedicated HTTP proxy server that has been placed behind another firewall system. The HTTP proxy would handle outbound connections to external web servers and possibly filter for active content. Requests from users first go to the proxy, and the proxy then sends the request (possibly changed) to the outside web server. The response from that web server then comes back to the proxy, which relays it to the user. Many organizations enable caching of frequently used web pages on the proxy to reduce network traffic and improve response times.

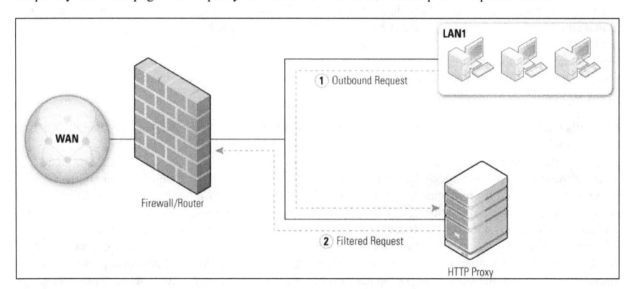

Figure 2-2. Application Proxy Configuration

2.1.6 Virtual Private Networking

Firewall devices at the edge of a network are sometimes required to do more than block unwanted traffic. A common requirement for these firewalls is to encrypt and decrypt specific network traffic flows between the protected network and external networks. This nearly always involves virtual private networks (VPN), which use additional protocols to encrypt traffic and provide user authentication and integrity checking. VPNs are most often used to provide secure network communications across untrusted networks. For example, VPN technology is widely used to extend the protected network of a multi-site organization across the Internet, and sometimes to provide secure remote user access to internal organizational networks via the Internet. Two common choices for secure VPNs are IPsec[6] and Secure Sockets Layer (SSL)/Transport Layer Security (TLS).[7]

The two most common VPN architectures are gateway-to-gateway and host-to-gateway.[8] Gateway-to-gateway architectures connect multiple fixed sites over public lines through the use of VPN gateways—for example, to connect branch offices to an organization's headquarters. A VPN gateway is usually part of another network device such as a firewall or router. When a VPN connection is established between the two gateways, users at branch locations are unaware of the connection and do not require any special settings on their computers. The second type of architecture, host-to-gateway, provides a secure connection to the network for individual users, usually called *remote users*, who are located outside of the organization (at home, in a hotel, etc.) Here, a client on the user machine negotiates the secure connection with the organization's VPN gateway.[9] For gateway-to-gateway and host-to-gateway VPNs, the VPN functionality is often part of the firewall itself. Placing it behind the firewall would require VPN traffic to be passed through the firewall while encrypted, preventing the firewall from inspecting the traffic.

All remote access (host-to-gateway) VPNs allow the firewall administrator to decide which users have access to which network resources. This access control is normally available on a per-user and per-group basis; that is, the VPN policy can specify which users and groups are authorized to access which resources, should an organization need that level of granularity. VPNs generally rely on authentication protocols such as Remote Authentication Dial In User Service (RADIUS).[10] RADIUS uses several different types of authentication credentials, with the most common examples being username and password, digital signatures, and hardware tokens. Another authentication protocol often used by VPNs is the Lightweight Directory Access Protocol (LDAP); it is particularly useful for making access decisions for individual users and groups.

To run VPN functionality on a firewall requires additional resources that depend on the amount of traffic flowing across the VPN and the type of encryption being used. For some environments, the added traffic associated with VPNs might require additional capacity planning and resources. Planning is also needed to determine the type of VPN (gateway-to-gateway and/or host-to-gateway) that should be included in the firewall. Many firewalls include hardware acceleration for encryption to minimize the impact of VPN services.

2.1.7 Network Access Control

Another common requirement for firewalls at the edge of a network is to perform client checks for incoming connections from remote users and allow or disallow access based on those checks. This checking, commonly called *network access control (NAC)* or *network access protection (NAP)*, allows access based on the user's credentials and the results of performing "health checks" on the user's computer. Health checks typically consist of verifying that one or more of the following comply with organizational policy:

---

[6] For additional information on IPsec, see NIST SP 800-77, *Guide to IPsec VPNs* (http://csrc.nist.gov/publications/PubsSPs.html).

[7] For additional information on SSL and TLS, see NIST SP 800-52, *Guidelines for the Selection and Use of Transport Layer Security (TLS) Implementations* and NIST SP 800-113, *Guide to SSL VPNs* (http://csrc.nist.gov/publications/PubsSPs.html).

[8] For additional information on VPN architectures, see NIST SP 800-77, *Guide to IPsec VPNs* and NIST SP 800-113, *Guide to SSL VPNs* (http://csrc.nist.gov/publications/PubsSPs.html).

[9] Host-to-gateway architectures usually require some user participation, such as initiating the VPN connection or providing credentials to the VPN for authentication.

[10] RADIUS is defined in RFC 2865 (http://www.rfc-editor.org/rfc/rfc2865.txt).

- Latest updates to antimalware and personal firewall software

- Configuration settings for antimalware and personal firewall software

- Elapsed time since the previous malware scan

- Patch level of the operating system and selected applications

- Security configuration of the operating system and selected applications

These health checks require software on the user's system that is controlled by the firewall. If the user has acceptable credentials but the device does not pass the health check, the user and device may get only limited access to the internal network for remediation purposes.

2.1.8   Unified Threat Management (UTM)

Many firewalls combine multiple features into a single system, the idea being that it is easier to set and maintain policy on a single system than on many systems that are deployed at the same location on a network. A typical unified threat management (UTM) system has a firewall, malware detection and eradication, sensing and blocking of suspicious network probes, and so on. There are pros and cons to merging multiple, not-completely-related functions into a single system. For example, deploying a UTM reduces complexity by making a single system responsible for multiple security objectives, but it also requires that the UTM have all the desired features to meet every one of the objectives. Another tradeoff is in performance: a single system handling multiple tasks has to have enough resources such as CPU speed and memory to handle every task assigned to it. Some organizations will find the balance favors a UTM, while other organizations will use multiple firewalls at the same location in their network.

2.1.9   Web Application Firewalls

The HTTP protocol used in web servers has been exploited by attackers in many ways, such as to place malicious software on the computer of someone browsing the web, or to fool a person into revealing private information that they might not have otherwise. Many of these exploits can be detected by specialized application firewalls called *web application firewalls* that reside in front of the web server.

Web application firewalls are a relatively new technology, as compared to other firewall technologies, and the type of threats that they mitigate are still changing frequently. Because they are put in front of web servers to prevent attacks on the server, they are often considered to be very different than traditional firewalls.

2.1.10 Firewalls for Virtual Infrastructures

Many virtualization solutions allow more than one operating system to run on a single computer simultaneously, each appearing as if it were a real computer. This has become popular recently because it allows organizations to make more efficient use of computer hardware. Most of these types of virtualization systems include *virtualized networking*, which allows the multiple operating systems to communicate as if they were on a standard Ethernet, even though there is no actual networking hardware.

Network activity that passes directly between virtualized operating systems within a host cannot be monitored by an external firewall. However, some virtualization systems offer built-in firewalls or allow third-party software firewalls to be added as plug-ins. Using firewalls to monitor virtualized networking is a relatively new area of firewall technology, and it is likely to change significantly as virtualization usage continues to increase.

2.2 Firewalls for Individual Hosts and Home Networks

Although firewalls at a network's perimeter provide some measure of protection for internal hosts, in many cases additional network protection is required. Network firewalls are not able to recognize all instances and forms of attack, allowing some attacks to penetrate and reach internal hosts—and attacks sent from one internal host to another may not even pass through a network firewall. Because of these and other factors, network designers often include firewall functionality at places other than the network perimeter to provide an additional layer of security. This section describes firewalls specifically designed for deployment onto individual hosts and home networks.

2.2.1 Host-Based Firewalls and Personal Firewalls

Host-based firewalls for servers and personal firewalls for desktop and laptop personal computers (PC) provide an additional layer of security against network-based attacks. These firewalls are software-based, residing on the hosts they are protecting—each monitors and controls the incoming and outgoing network traffic for a single host. They can provide more granular protection than network firewalls to meet the needs of specific hosts.

Host-based firewalls are available as part of server operating systems such as Linux, Windows, Solaris, BSD, and Mac OS X Server, and they can also be installed as third-party add-ons. Configuring a host-based firewall to allow only necessary traffic to the server provides protection against malicious activity from all hosts, including those on the same subnet or on other internal subnets not separated by a network firewall. Limiting outgoing traffic from a server may also be helpful in preventing certain malware that infects a host from spreading to other hosts.[11] Host-based firewalls usually perform logging, and can often be configured to perform address-based and application-based access controls. Many host-based firewalls can also act as intrusion prevention systems (IPS) that, after detecting an attack in progress, take actions to thwart the attacker and prevent damage to the targeted host.

A personal firewall is software that runs on a desktop or laptop PC with a user-focused operating system such as Microsoft Windows Vista or Macintosh OS X. A personal firewall is similar to a host-based firewall, but because the computer being protected is meant for end users, the interface is usually different (and presumably easier for the typical user to understand). A personal firewall provides an additional layer of security for PCs located both inside and outside perimeter firewalls (e.g., mobile laptop users), because it can restrict inbound communications and can often limit outbound communications as well. This not only allows personal firewalls to protect PCs from incoming attacks, but also limits the spread of malware from infected PCs and the use of unauthorized software such as peer-to-peer file sharing utilities. Personal firewalls are often packaged with antimalware programs, intrusion detection software, and other security utilities.[12]

Some personal firewalls allow creation of different profiles based on location, such as a profile for use inside the organization's network and a different profile for use when at a remote location. This is particularly important when a computer is used on an untrusted external network, because having a separate firewall profile for use on such networks can restrict network activity more tightly and provide stronger protection than having a single profile for all networks.

---

[11] If an attacker compromises a host and gains administrator-level privileges, the attacker can disable or circumvent the host-based firewall.

[12] For additional information about personal firewalls, see NIST SP 800-114, *User's Guide to Securing External Devices for Telework and Remote Access* (http://csrc.nist.gov/publications/PubsSPs.html).

In addition to traditional stateful filtering, many personal firewalls can be configured to allow communications based on lists of authorized applications—such as web browsers contacting web servers and email clients sending and receiving email messages—and to deny communications involving any other applications. These are referred to as *application-based firewalls*. Access control is based on the applications or services launched, and not on the ports or services.

Management of personal firewalls should be centralized if at all possible to help efficiently create, distribute, and enforce policies for all users and groups. Doing this will ensure that the organization's security policy will be in effect whenever a user is accessing the organization's computing resources. But regardless of whether a personal firewall is managed by central administrators or individual users, any warning messages that are generated by the firewall should be shown to the user of the PC to help them rectify problems that are found.

2.2.2 Personal Firewall Appliances

In addition to using personal firewalls on their PCs, some teleworkers also use a small, inexpensive device called a firewall appliance or firewall router to protect the computers on their home networks. A personal firewall appliance performs functions similar to a personal firewall, including some of the more advanced features listed earlier in this section—such as VPN. Even if each computer on a home network is using a personal firewall, a firewall appliance is still a valuable added layer of security. Should a personal firewall on a computer malfunction, be disabled, or be misconfigured, the firewall appliance can still protect the computer from unauthorized network communications from external computers. Personal firewall appliances are essentially like small enterprise firewalls that are deployed away from the organization, so the ability to perform central management and administration is as important for personal firewall appliances as it is for enterprise firewalls.[13]

Some personal firewall appliances can be partially configured by Universal Plug and Play (UPnP), which allows applications on PCs behind the firewall to automatically ask the firewall to open certain ports so that the applications can have two-way communications with an external system. Most personal firewalls that support dynamic reconfiguration via UPnP have this featured turned off by default because it is a significant security risk to allow untrusted applications to alter a firewall's security policy.

2.3 Limitations of Firewall Inspection

Firewalls can only work effectively on traffic that they can inspect. Regardless of the firewall technology chosen, a firewall that cannot understand the traffic flowing through it will not handle that traffic properly—for example, allowing traffic that should be blocked. Many network protocols use cryptography to hide the contents of the traffic. Section 2.1.6 covered IPsec and TLS; other encrypting protocols include Secure Shell (SSH) and Secure Real-time Transport Protocol (SRTP). Firewalls also cannot read application data that is encrypted, such as email that is encrypted using the S/MIME or OpenPGP protocols, or files that are manually encrypted. Another limitation faced by some firewalls is understanding traffic that is tunneled, even if it is not encrypted. For example, IPv6 traffic can be tunneled in IPv4 in many different ways. The content may still be unencrypted, but if the firewall does not understand the particular tunneling mechanism used, the traffic cannot be interpreted.

In all these cases, the firewall's rules will determine what to do with traffic it does not (or, in the case of encrypted traffic, cannot) understand. An organization should have policies about how to handle traffic in such cases, such as either permitting or blocking encrypted traffic that is not authorized to be encrypted.

---

[13] Additional information on personal firewall appliances is available from NIST SP 800-114.

2.4 Summary of Recommendations

The following items summarize the major recommendations from this section:

- The use of NAT should be considered a form of routing, not a type of firewall.

- Organizations should only permit outbound traffic that uses the source IP addresses in use by the organization.

- Compliance checking is only useful in a firewall when it can block communication that can be harmful to protected systems.

- When choosing the type of firewall to deploy, it is important to decide whether the firewall needs to act as an application proxy.

- Management of personal firewalls should be centralized to help efficiently create, distribute, and enforce policies for all users and groups.

3. Firewalls and Network Architectures

Firewalls are used to separate networks with differing security requirements, such as the Internet and an internal network that houses servers with sensitive data. Organizations should use firewalls wherever their internal networks and systems interface with external networks and systems, and where security requirements vary among their internal networks. This section is intended to help organizations determine where firewalls should be placed, and where other networks and systems should be located in relation to the firewalls.

Since one of the primary functions of a firewall is to prevent unwanted traffic from entering a network (and, in some cases, from exiting it), firewalls should be placed at the edge of logical network boundaries.[14] This normally means that firewalls are positioned either as a node where the network splits into multiple paths, or inline along a single path. In routed networks, the firewall usually resides just on the network at the location immediately before traffic enters the router (the *ingress* point), and is sometimes co-resident with the router. It is rare to place the firewall for a multi-path node after the router because the firewall device would need to watch each of the multiple exit paths that typically exist in such situations. The vast majority of hardware firewall devices contain router capabilities, and in switched networks, a firewall is often part of the switch itself to enable it to protect as many of the switched segments as possible.

Firewall vendors often vary in their terminology for the logical flow of firewall traffic. A firewall takes traffic that has not been checked, checks it against the firewall's policy, and then acts accordingly (e.g., passes the traffic, blocks it, passes it with some modification). Because all traffic on a network has a direction, policies are based on the direction that the traffic is moving. For the purposes of this document, traffic that has not yet been checked is coming from the "unprotected side" of the firewall and is moving towards the "protected side." Some firewalls check traffic in both directions—for example, if they are set up to prevent specific traffic from an organization's local area network (LAN) from escaping to the Internet.[15] In these cases, the protected side of the firewall is the one facing the outside network.

Section 2 lists many different types of firewall technologies. Network firewalls are almost always hardware devices with multiple network interfaces; host-based and personal firewalls involve software that resides on a single computer and protects only that computer; and personal firewall appliances are designed to protect a single PC or a small office/home office network. This section focuses on network firewalls because the other types are usually unrelated to network topology issues.

3.1 Network Layouts with Firewalls

Figure 3-1 shows a typical network layout with a hardware firewall device acting as a router. The unprotected side of the firewall connects to the single path labeled "WAN," and the protected side connects to three paths labeled "LAN1," "LAN2," and "LAN3." The firewall acts as a router for traffic between the wide area network (WAN) path and the LAN paths. In the figure, one of the LAN paths also has a router; some organizations prefer to use multiple layers of routers due to legacy routing policies within the network.

---

[14] In addition to traditional network boundaries, this also includes boundaries related to the use of virtual machines. For example, there may be a need to restrict network activity between two virtual machines with different security policies.

[15] Some firewalls are configured to permit traffic in only one direction—for example, a firewall set up as a guard to allow limited traffic flows from a higher-impact system to a lower-impact system, but no traffic initiated by the lower-impact system to reach the higher-impact system.

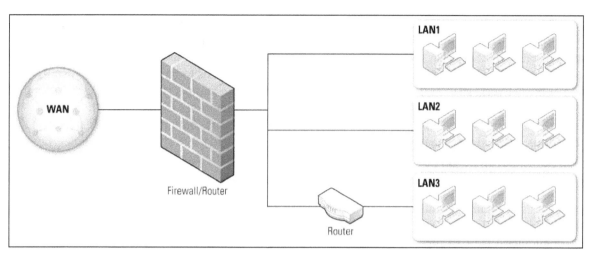

Figure 3-1. Simple Routed Network with Firewall Device

Many hardware firewall devices have a feature called *DMZ*, an acronym related to the demilitarized zones that are sometimes set up between warring countries. While no single technical definition exists for firewall DMZs, they are usually interfaces on a routing firewall that are similar to the interfaces found on the firewall's protected side. The major difference is that traffic moving between the DMZ and other interfaces on the protected side of the firewall still goes through the firewall and can have firewall protection policies applied. DMZs are sometimes useful for organizations that have hosts that need to have all traffic destined for the host bypass some of the firewall's policies (for example, because the DMZ hosts are sufficiently hardened), but traffic coming from the hosts to other systems on the organization's network need to go through the firewall. It is common to put public-facing servers, such as web and email servers, on the DMZ. An example of this is shown in Figure 3-2, a simple network layout of a firewall with a DMZ. Traffic from the Internet goes into the firewall and is routed to systems on the firewall's protected side or to systems on the DMZ. Traffic between systems on the DMZ and systems on the protected network goes through the firewall, and can have firewall policies applied.

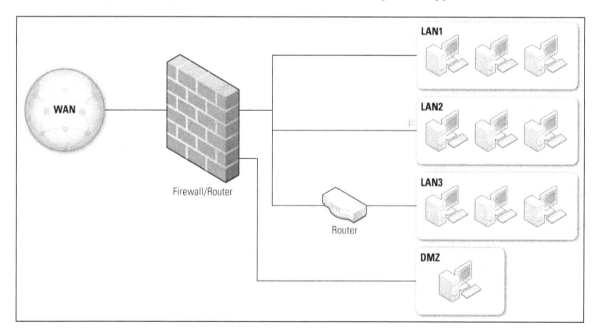

Figure 3-2. Firewall with a DMZ

Most network architectures are hierarchical, meaning that a single path from an outside network splits into multiple paths on the inside network—and it is generally most efficient to place a firewall at the node where the paths split. This has the advantage of positioning the firewall where there is no question as to what is "outside" and what is "inside." However, there may be reasons to have additional firewalls on the inside of the network, such as to protect one set of computers from another. If a network's architecture is not hierarchical, the same firewall policies should be used on all ingresses to the network. In many organizations, there is only supposed to be one ingress to the network, but other ingresses are set up on an ad-hoc basis, often in ways that are not allowed by overall policy. In these situations, if a properly configured firewall is not placed at each entry point, malicious traffic that would normally be blocked by the main ingress can enter the network by other means.

The diagrams in Figures 3-1 and 3-2 each show a single firewall; however, many implementations use multiple firewalls. Some vendors sell *high-availability* (*HA*) firewalls, which allow one firewall to take over for another if the first firewall fails or is taken offline for maintenance. HA firewalls are deployed in pairs at the same spot in the network topology so that they both have the same external and internal connections. While HA firewalls can increase reliability, they can also introduce some problems, such as the need to combine logs between the paired firewalls and possible confusion by administrators when configuring the firewalls (for example, knowing which firewall is pushing its policy changes to the other firewall). HA functionality may be provided through a variety of vendor-specific techniques.

3.2   Firewalls Acting as Network Address Translators

Most firewalls can perform NAT, which is sometimes called port address translation (PAT) or network address and port translation (NAPT). Despite the popular misconception, NAT is not part of the security functionality of a firewall. The security benefit of NAT—preventing a host outside the firewall from initiating contact with a host behind NAT—can just as easily be achieved by a stateful firewall with less disruption to protocols that do not work as well behind NAT. However, turning on a firewall's NAT feature is usually easier than properly configuring the firewall policy to have the same protections, so many people think of NATs as primarily a security feature.

Typically, a NAT acts as a router that has a network with private addresses on the inside and a single public address on the outside. The way a NAT performs this many-to-one mapping varies between implementations, but almost always involves the following:

■ Hosts on the inside network initiating connections to the outside network cause the NAT to map the source port of the connection to a different source port that is controlled by the NAT. The NAT uses this source port number to map connections from the outside back to the host on the inside.

■ Hosts on the outside of the network cannot initiate contact with hosts on the inside network. In some firewalls, the NAT can be configured to map a particular destination port on the NAT to a particular host on the inside of the NAT; for example, all HTTP requests that go to the NAT could be directed to a single host on the protected side of the firewall. This feature is sometimes called *pinholing*.

Although NATs are not in and of themselves security features of a firewall, they interact with the firewall's security policy. For example, any policy that requires that all HTTP servers accessible to the outside be on the DMZ must prevent the NAT from pinholing TCP port 80. Another example of where NATs interact with security policy is the ability to identify the source of traffic in a firewall's logs. If a NAT is used, it must report the private address in the logs instead of the translated public address, otherwise the logs will incorrectly identify many hosts by the single public address.

3.3 Architecture with Multiple Layers of Firewalls

There is no limitation on where a firewall can be placed in a network. While firewalls should be at the edge of a logical network boundary, creating an "inside" and "outside" on either side of the firewall, a network administrator may wish to have additional boundaries within the network and deploy additional firewalls to establish such boundaries. The use of multiple layers of firewalls is quite common to provide defense-in-depth. An example of this was mentioned in Section 2.2.1, where a host-based firewall creates a boundary just before the host it is installed upon and adds another set of firewall policies to the architecture of the network. Using multiple layers of network firewalls is another common technique.

A typical situation that requires multiple layers of network firewalls is the presence of internal users with varying levels of trust. For example, an organization might want to protect its accounting databases from being accessed by users who are not part of the accounting department. This could be accomplished by placing one firewall at the edge of the network (to prevent general access to the network from the Internet) and another at the edge of the internal network that defines the boundary of the accounting department. The inner firewall would block access to the database server by anyone outside the accounting network while allowing limited access to other resources on the accounting network. Another typical use for firewalls inside a network with a firewall at its edge involves visitors who need access to the Internet. Many organizations deploy specific wireless access points within their networks for visitor use. A firewall between the access points and the rest of the internal network can prevent visitors from accessing the local network with the same privileges as an employee.

Placing a firewall within a network that already has one at the edge requires good planning and policy coordination to prevent inadvertent security lapses. When designing policies for an inner firewall, the administrator could make assumptions that result in poor policy choices—for example, if the inner firewall's administrator assumes that the outer firewall is already preventing certain types of traffic from reaching the inner firewall, and the outer firewall's administrator later modifies existing policy, hosts behind the inner firewall will be exposed to additional threats. A better approach is to duplicate outer firewall policies that are also relevant for inner firewalls on each inner firewall. This may be difficult if these firewalls are not able to coordinate their policies automatically, which is particularly likely when firewalls are from different manufacturers.

Another common problem with using multiple layers of network firewalls is the increased difficulty it presents in tracing firewall problems. If one firewall stands between a user and a server, and the user cannot connect to the server, it is easy to check that firewall's logs to see if the connection is being permitted. But if multiple firewalls are involved, the problem becomes more difficult because an administrator must locate all firewalls in the chain and check their logs to find where the problem originates. The presence of multiple layers of application-proxy gateways is particularly daunting, because each gateway can change a message, which makes debugging even more difficult.

3.4 Summary of Recommendations

The following items summarize the major recommendations from this section:

- In general, a firewall should fit into a current network's layout. However, an organization might change its network architecture at the same time as it deploys a firewall as part of an overall security upgrade.

- Different common network architectures lead to very different choices for where to place a firewall, so an organization should assess which architecture works best for its security goals.

■ If an edge firewall has a DMZ, consider which outward-facing services should be run from the DMZ and which should remain on the inside network.

■ Do not rely on NATs to provide the benefits of firewalls.

■ In some environments, putting one firewall behind another may lead to a desired security goal, but in general such multiple layers of firewalls can be troublesome.

4. Firewall Policy

A firewall policy dictates how firewalls should handle network traffic for specific IP addresses and address ranges, protocols, applications, and content types (e.g., active content) based on the organization's information security policies. Before a firewall policy is created, some form of risk analysis should be performed to develop a list of the types of traffic needed by the organization and categorize how they must be secured—including which types of traffic can traverse a firewall under what circumstances.[16] This risk analysis should be based on an evaluation of threats; vulnerabilities; countermeasures in place to mitigate vulnerabilities; and the impact if systems or data are compromised. Firewall policy should be documented in the system security plan and maintained and updated frequently as classes of new attacks or vulnerabilities arise, or as the organization's needs regarding network applications change. The policy should also include specific guidance on how to address changes to the ruleset.

Generally, firewalls should block all inbound and outbound traffic that has not been expressly permitted by the firewall policy—traffic that is not needed by the organization. This practice, known as *deny by default*, decreases the risk of attack and can also reduce the volume of traffic carried on the organization's networks. Because of the dynamic nature of hosts, networks, protocols, and applications, deny by default is a more secure approach than permitting all traffic that is not explicitly forbidden.

This section provides details on what types of traffic should be blocked. Section 4.1 discusses policies for packet filtering and stateful inspection based on IP addresses and other IP characteristics. Section 4.2 covers policies relating to application-specific traffic. Section 4.3 covers access based on user identity, and Section 4.4 describes policies triggered by network activity.

4.1 Policies Based on IP Addresses and Protocols

Firewall policies should only allow necessary IP protocols through. Examples of commonly used IP protocols, with their IP protocol numbers,[17] are ICMP (1), TCP (6), and UDP (17). Other IP protocols, such as IPsec components Encapsulating Security Payload (ESP) (50) and Authentication Header (AH) (51) and routing protocols, may also need to pass through firewalls. These necessary protocols should be restricted whenever possible to the specific hosts and networks within the organization with a need to use them. By permitting only necessary protocols, all unnecessary IP protocols are denied by default.

Some IP protocols are rarely passed between an outside network and an organization's LAN, and therefore can simply be blocked in both directions at the firewall. For example, IGMP is a protocol used to control multicast networks, but multicast is rarely used, and when it is, it is often not used across the Internet. Therefore, blocking all IGMP traffic in both directions is feasible if multicast is not used.

4.1.1 IP Addresses and Other IP Characteristics

Firewall policies should only permit appropriate source and destination IP addresses to be used. Specific recommendations for IP addresses include:

■ Traffic with invalid source or destination addresses should always be blocked, regardless of the firewall location. Examples of relatively common invalid IPv4 addresses are 127.0.0.0 to

---

[16] The process to perform a risk assessment and create this type of list is not detailed here. For additional information, see NIST SP 800-30, *Risk Management Guide for Information Technology Systems*, and SP 800-18 Revision 1, *Guide for Developing Security Plans for Federal Information Systems*, at http://csrc.nist.gov/publications/PubsSPs.html.
[17] IP protocol number assignments are defined in http://www.iana.org/assignments/protocol-numbers.

127.255.255.255 (also known as the *localhost* addresses) and 0.0.0.0 (interpreted by some operating systems as a localhost or a broadcast address). These have no legitimate use on a network. Also, traffic using link-local addresses (169.254.0.0 to 169.254.255.255) should be blocked.

■ Traffic with an invalid source address for incoming traffic or destination address for outgoing traffic (an invalid "external" address) should be blocked at the network perimeter. This traffic is often caused by malware, spoofing, denial of service attacks, or misconfigured equipment. The most common type of invalid external addresses is an IPv4 address within the ranges in RFC 1918, *Address Allocation for Private Internets*, that are reserved for private networks. These ranges are 10.0.0.0 to 10.255.255.255 (10.0.0.0/8 in Classless Inter-Domain Routing [CIDR] notation), 172.16.0.0 to 172.31.255.255 (172.16.0.0/12), and 192.168.0.0 to 192.168.255.255 (192.168.0.0/16).

■ Traffic with a private destination address for incoming traffic or source address for outgoing traffic (an "internal" address) should be blocked at the network perimeter. Perimeter devices can perform address translation services to permit internal hosts with private addresses to communicate through the perimeter, but private addresses should not be passed through the network perimeter.

■ Outbound traffic with invalid source addresses should be blocked (this is often called *egress filtering*). Systems that have been compromised by attackers can be used to attack other systems on the Internet; using invalid source addresses makes these kinds of attacks more difficult to stop. Blocking this type of traffic at an organization's firewall helps reduce the effectiveness of these attacks.

■ Incoming traffic with a destination address of the firewall itself should be blocked unless the firewall is offering services for incoming traffic that require direct connections—for example, if the firewall is acting as an application proxy.

Organizations should also block the following types of traffic at the perimeter:

■ Traffic containing IP source routing information, which allows a system to specify the routes that packets will employ while traveling from source to destination. This could potentially permit an attacker to construct a packet that bypasses network security controls. IP source routing is rarely used on modern networks, and valid applications are even less common on the Internet.

■ Traffic from outside the network containing broadcast addresses that is directed to inside the network. Any system that responds to the directed broadcast will then send its response to the system specified by the source, rather than to the source system itself. These packets can be used to create huge "storms" of network traffic for denial of service attacks. Regular broadcast addresses, as well as addresses used for multicast IP, may or may not be appropriate for blocking at an organization's firewall. Multicast and broadcast networking is seldom used in normal networking environments, but when it is used both inside and outside of the organization, it should be allowed through firewalls.

Firewalls at the network perimeter should block all incoming traffic to networks and hosts that should not be accessible from external networks. These firewalls should also block all outgoing traffic from the organization's networks and hosts that should not be permitted to access external networks. Deciding which addresses should be blocked is often one of the most time-consuming aspects of developing firewall IP policies. It is also one of the most error-prone, because the IP address associated with an undesired entity often changes over time.

4.1.2 IPv6

IPv6 is a new version of IP that is increasingly being deployed. Although IPv6's internal format and address length differ from those of IPv4, many other features remain the same—and some of these are relevant to firewalls. For the features that are the same between IPv4 and IPv6, firewalls should work the same. For example, blocking all inbound and outbound traffic that has not been expressly permitted by the firewall policy should be done regardless of whether or not the traffic has an IPv4 or IPv6 address.

As of this writing, some firewalls cannot handle IPv6 traffic at all; others are able to handle it but have limited abilities to filter IPv6 traffic; and still others can filter IPv6 traffic to approximately the same extent as IPv4 traffic. Every organization, whether or not it allows IPv6 traffic to enter its internal network, needs a firewall that is capable of filtering this traffic. These firewalls should have the following capabilities:

■ The firewall should be able to use IPv6 addresses in all filtering rules that use IPv4 addresses.

■ The administrative interface should allow administrators to clone IPv4 rules to IPv6 addresses to make administration easier.

■ The firewall needs to be able to filter ICMPv6, as specified in RFC 4890, *Recommendations for Filtering ICMPv6 Messages in Firewalls*.

■ The firewall should be able to block IPv6-related protocols such as 6-to-4 and 4-to-6 tunneling, Teredo, and Intra-site Automatic Tunnel Addressing Protocol (ISATAP) if they are not required.

■ Many sites tunnel IPv6 packets in IPv4 packets. This is particularly common for sites experimenting with IPv6, because it is currently easier to obtain IPv6 transit from a *tunnel broker* through a v6-to-v4 tunnel than to get native IPv6 transit from an Internet service provider (ISP). A number of ways exist to do this, and standards for tunneling are still evolving. If the firewall is able to inspect the contents of IPv4 packets, it needs to know how to inspect traffic for any tunneling method used by the organization. A corollary to this is that if an organization is using a firewall to prohibit IPv6 coming into or going out of its network, that firewall needs to recognize and block all forms of v6-to-v4 tunneling.

Note that the above list is short and not all the rules are security-specific. Because IPv6 deployment is still in its early stages, there is not yet widespread agreement in the IPv6 operations community about what an IPv6 firewall should do that is different from IPv4 firewalls.

For firewalls that permit IPv6 use, traffic with invalid source or destination IPv6 addresses should always be blocked—this is similar to blocking traffic with invalid IPv4 addresses. Since much more effort has been spent on making lists of invalid IPv4 addresses than on IPv6 addresses, finding lists of invalid IPv6 addresses can be difficult. Also, IPv6 allows network administrators to allocate addresses in their assigned ranges in different ways. This means that in a particular address range assigned to an organization, there can literally be trillions of invalid IPv6 addresses and only a few that are valid. By necessity, listing which IPv6 addresses are invalid will have to be less fine-grained than listing invalid IPv4 addresses, and the firewall rules that use these lists will be less effective than their IPv4 counterparts.

Organizations that do not yet use IPv6 should block all native and tunneled IPv6 traffic at their firewalls. Note that such blocking limits testing and evaluation of IPv6 and IPv6 tunneling technologies for future deployment. To permit such use, the firewall administrator can selectively unblock IPv6 or the specific tunneling technologies of interest for use by the authorized testers.

4.1.3   TCP and UDP

Application protocols can use TCP, UDP, or both, depending on the design of the protocol. An application server typically listens on one or more fixed TCP or UDP ports. Some applications use a single port, but many applications use multiple ports. For example, although SMTP uses TCP port 25 for sending mail, it uses TCP port 587 for mail submission. Similarly, FTP uses at least two ports, one of which can be unpredictable, and while most web servers use only TCP port 80, it is common to have web sites that also use additional ports such as TCP port 8080. Some applications use both TCP and UDP; for example, DNS lookups can occur on UDP port 53 or TCP port 53. Application clients typically use any of a wide range of ports.

As with other aspects of firewall rulesets, deny by default policies should be used for incoming TCP and UDP traffic. Less stringent policies are generally used for outgoing TCP and UDP traffic because most organizations permit their users to access a wide range of external applications located on millions of external hosts.

In addition to allowing and blocking UDP and TCP traffic, many firewalls are also able to report or block malformed UDP and TCP traffic directed towards the firewall or to hosts protected by the firewall. This traffic is frequently used to scan for hosts, and may also be used in certain types of attacks. The firewall can help block such activity—or at least report when such activity is happening.

4.1.4   ICMP

Attackers can use various ICMP types and codes to perform reconnaissance or manipulate the flow of network traffic.[18] However, ICMP is needed for many useful things, such as getting reasonable performance across the Internet. Some firewall policies block all ICMP traffic, but this often leads to problems with diagnostics and performance. Other common policies allow all outgoing ICMP traffic, but limit incoming ICMP to those types and codes needed for Path Maximum Transmission Unit (PMTU) discovery (ICMP code 3) and destination reachability.

To prevent malicious activity, firewalls at the network perimeter should deny all incoming and outgoing ICMP traffic except for those types and codes specifically permitted by the organization. For ICMP in IPv4, ICMP type 3 messages should not be filtered because they are used for important network diagnostics. The *ping* command (ICMP code 8) is an important network diagnostic, but incoming pings are often blocked by firewall policies to prevent attackers from learning more about the internal topology of the organization's network. For ICMP in IPv6, many types of messages must be allowed in specific circumstances to enable various IPv6 features. See RFC 4890, *Recommendations for Filtering ICMPv6 Messages in Firewalls*, for detailed information on selecting which ICMPv6 types to allow or disallow for a particular firewall type.

ICMP is often used by low-level networking protocols to increase the speed and reliability of networking. Therefore, ICMP within an organization's network generally should not be blocked by firewalls that are not at the perimeter of the network, unless security needs outweigh network operational needs. Similarly, if an organization has more than one network, ICMP that comes from or goes to other networks within the organization should not be blocked.

---

[18]   ICMP type and code numbers are defined at http://www.iana.org/assignments/icmp-parameters.

4.1.5 IPsec Protocols

An organization needs to have a policy whether or not to allow IPsec VPNs that start or end inside its network perimeter. The ESP and AH protocols are used for IPsec VPNs, and a firewall that blocks these protocols will not allow IPsec VPNs to pass. While blocking ESP can hinder the use of encryption to protect sensitive data, it can also force users who would normally encrypt their data with ESP to allow it to be inspected—for example, by a stateful inspection firewall or an application-proxy gateway.

Organizations that allow IPsec VPNs should block ESP and AH except to and from specific addresses on the internal network—those addresses belong to IPsec gateways that are allowed to be VPN endpoints.[19] Enforcing this policy will require people inside the organization to obtain the appropriate policy approval to open ESP and/or AH access to their IPsec routers. This will also reduce the amount of encrypted traffic coming from inside the network that cannot be examined by network security controls.

4.2   Policies Based on Applications

Most early firewall work involved simply blocking unwanted or suspicious traffic at the network boundary. Inbound application firewalls or application proxies take a different approach—they let traffic destined for a particular server into the network, but capture that traffic in a server that processes it like a port-based firewall. The application-based approach provides an additional layer of security for incoming traffic by validating some of the traffic before it reaches the desired server. The theory is that the inbound application firewall's or proxy's additional security layer can protect the server better than the server can protect itself—and can also remove malicious traffic before it reaches the server to help reduce server load. In some cases, an application firewall or proxy can remove traffic that the server might not be able to remove on its own because it has greater filtering capabilities. An application firewall or proxy also prevents the server from having direct access to the outside network.

If possible, inbound application firewalls and proxies should be used in front of any server that does not have sufficient security features to protect it from application-specific attacks. The main considerations when deciding whether or not to use an inbound application firewall or proxy are:

- Is a suitable application firewall available? Or, if appropriate, is a suitable application proxy available?

- Is the server already sufficiently protected by existing firewalls?

- Can the main server remove malicious content as effectively as the application firewall or proxy?

- Is the latency caused by an application proxy acceptable for the application?

- How easy it is to update the filtering rules on the main server and the application firewall or proxy to handle newly developed threats?

Application proxies can introduce problems if they are not highly capable. Unless an application proxy is significantly more robust than the server and easy to keep updated, it is usually best to stay with the application server alone. Application firewalls can also introduce problems if they are not fast enough to handle the traffic destined for the server. However, it is also important to consider the server's resources—if the server does not have sufficient resources to withstand attacks, the application firewall or proxy could be used as a shield.

---

[19]   Wherever there is a policy to allow ESP and/or AH traffic through a firewall, it is extremely likely that the firewall also needs a policy to allow Internet Key Exchange (IKE) traffic as well. IKE runs on UDP port 500, and it can also use UDP port 4500 for IPsec systems that support NAT traversal.

When an inbound application firewall or proxy is behind a perimeter firewall or in the firewall's DMZ, the perimeter firewall should be blocking based on IP addresses, as described earlier in this section, to reduce the load on the application firewall or proxy. Doing this puts more of the address-specific policy in a single place—the main firewall—and reduces the amount of traffic seen by the application firewall or proxy, freeing more power to filter content. Of course, if the perimeter firewall is also the application firewall and an internal application proxy is not used, no such rules are needed.

Outbound application proxies are useful for detecting systems that are making inappropriate or dangerous connections from inside the protected network. By far the most common type of outbound proxy is for HTTP. Outbound HTTP proxies allow an organization to filter dangerous content before it reaches the requesting PC. They also help an organization better understand and log web traffic from its users, and to detect activity that is being tunneled over HTTP. When an HTTP proxy filters content, it can alert the web user that the site being visited sent the filtered content. The most prominent non-security benefit of HTTP proxies is caching web pages for increased speed and decreased bandwidth use. Most organizations should employ HTTP proxies.

4.3 Policies Based on User Identity

Traditional packet filtering does not see the identities of the users who are communicating in the traffic traversing the firewall, so firewall technologies without more advanced capabilities cannot have policies that allow or deny access based on those identities. However, many other firewall technologies can see these identities and therefore enact policies based on user authentication. One of the most common ways to enforce user identity policy at a firewall is by using a VPN. Both IPsec VPNs and SSL VPNs have many ways to authenticate users, such as with secrets that are provisioned on a user-by-user basis, with multi-factor authentication (e.g., time-based cryptographic tokens protected with PINs), or with digital certificates controlled by each user. NAC has also become a popular method for firewalls to allow or deny users access to particular network resources. In addition, application firewalls and proxies can allow or deny access to users based on the user authentication within the applications themselves.

Firewalls that enforce policies based on user identity should be able to reflect these policies in their logs. That is, it is probably not useful to only log the IP address from which a particular user connected if the user was allowed in by a user-specific policy; it is also important to log the user's identity as well.

4.4 Policies Based on Network Activity

Many firewalls allow the administrator to block established connections after a certain period of inactivity. For example, if a user on the outside of a firewall has logged into a file server but has not made any requests during the past 15 minutes, the policy might be to block any further traffic on that connection. Time-based policies are useful in thwarting attacks caused by a logged-in user walking away from a computer and someone else sitting down and using the established connections (and therefore the logged-in user's credentials). However, these policies can also be bothersome for users who make connections but do not use them frequently. For instance, a user might connect to a file server to read a file and then spend a long time editing the file. If the user does not save the file back to the file server before the firewall-mandated timeout, the timeout could cause the changes to the file to be lost.

Some organizations have mandates about when firewalls should block connections that are considered to be inactive, when applications should disconnect sessions if there is no activity, etc. A firewall used by such an organization should be able to set policies that match the mandates while being specific enough to match the security objective of the mandates.

A different type of firewall policy based on network activity is one that throttles or redirects traffic if the rate of traffic matching the policy rule is too high. For example, a firewall might redirect the connections made to a particular inside address to a slower route if the rate of connections is above a certain threshold. Another policy might be to drop incoming ICMP packets if the rate is too high. Crafting such policies is quite difficult because throttling and redirecting can cause desired traffic to be lost or have difficult-to-diagnose transient failures.

4.5 Summary of Recommendations

The following items summarize the major recommendations from this section:

■ An organization's firewall policy should be based on a comprehensive risk analysis.

■ Firewall policies should be based on blocking all inbound and outbound traffic, with exceptions made for desired traffic.

■ Policies should take into account the source and destination of the traffic in addition to the content.

■ Many types of IPv4 traffic, such as that with invalid or private addresses, should be blocked by default.

■ Organizations should have policies for handling incoming and outgoing IPv6 traffic.

■ An organization should determine which applications may send traffic into or out of its network and make firewall policies to block traffic for other applications.

5. Firewall Planning and Implementation

This section focuses on the planning and implementation of firewalls in the enterprise. As with any new technology deployment, firewall planning and implementation should be addressed in a phased approach. A successful firewall deployment can be achieved by following a clear, step-by-step planning and implementation process. The use of a phased approach for deployment can minimize unforeseen issues and identify potential pitfalls early on. This section explores in depth each of the firewall planning and implementation phases, including:

1. **Plan.** The first phase of the process involves identifying all requirements that an organization should consider when determining which firewall to implement to enforce the organization's security policy.

2. **Configure**. The second phase involves all facets of configuring the firewall platform. This includes installing hardware and software as well as setting up rules for the system.

3. **Test.** The next phase involves implementing and testing a prototype of the designed solution in a lab or test environment. The primary goals of testing are to evaluate the functionality, performance, scalability, and security of the solution, and to identify any issues—such as interoperability—with components.

4. **Deploy**. Once testing is completed and all issues are resolved, the next phase focuses on deployment of the firewall into the enterprise.

5. **Manage**. After the firewall has been deployed, it is managed throughout its lifecycle to include component maintenance and support for operational issues. This lifecycle process is repeated when enhancements or significant changes need to be incorporated into the solution.

5.1   Plan

The planning phase for choosing and implementing a firewall should begin only after an organization has determined that a firewall is needed to enforce the organization's security policy. This typically occurs following a risk assessment of the overall system. A risk assessment includes (1) the identification of threats and vulnerabilities in the information system; (2) the potential impact or magnitude of harm that a loss of confidentiality, integrity, or availability would have on the organization's assets or operations (including mission, function, image, or reputation) in the event of a threat exploitation of identified vulnerabilities; and (3) the identification and analysis of security controls for the information system[20].

Basic principles that organizations should follow in the planning of firewall deployments include:

■ **Use devices as they were intended to be used.** Firewalls should not be constructed of equipment not meant for firewall use. For example, routers are meant to handle routing, not highly complex filtering, which can cause an excess burden on the router's processor. Additionally, firewalls should not be expected to provide non-security services, such as acting as a web server or email server.

■ **Create defense-in-depth.** Defense-in-depth involves creating multiple layers of security. This allows risk to be better managed, because if one layer of defense becomes compromised, another layer is there to contain the attack. In the case of firewalls, defense-in-depth can be accomplished by using multiple firewalls throughout an organization, including at the perimeter, in front of sensitive internal departments, and on individual computers. For defense-in-depth to be truly effective, firewalls should

---

[20]   For additional information about risk assessments, see NIST SP 800-30, *Risk Management Guide for Information Technology Systems* (http://csrc.nist.gov/publications/PubsSPs.html).

be part of an overall security program that also includes products such as antimalware and intrusion detection software.

■ **Pay attention to internal threats.** Focusing attention solely on external threats leaves the network wide open to attacks from within. These threats may not come directly from insiders, but can involve internal hosts infected by malware or otherwise compromised by external attackers. Important internal systems should be placed behind internal firewalls.

■ **Document the firewall's capabilities.** Each model of firewall has different capabilities and limitations. These will sometimes affect the planning of the organization's security policy and firewall deployment strategy. Any features that positively or negatively affect this planning should be written into the overall planning document.

Keep in mind that the expression "all rules are meant to be broken" applies when building firewalls. While firewall implementers should keep the above rules in mind during planning, every network and organization has unique requirements and idiosyncrasies that could require unique solutions.

Organizations should consider the following when purchasing and implementing a firewall solution:

■ Security Capabilities

- Which areas of the organization need to be protected (the perimeter, internal departments, remote office, individual hosts, specific services, mobile clients, etc.)?

- Which types of firewall technologies will best address the kinds of traffic that need to be protected (packet filtering, stateful inspection, application firewall, application-proxy gateway, etc.)?

- What additional security features—such as intrusion detection capabilities, VPNs, and content filtering—does the firewall need to support?

■ Management

- Which protocols does the firewall support for remote management, such as HTTP-over-SSL, SSH, and access over a serial cable?

- Are any of the firewall's remote management protocols acceptable for use, according to the organization's policies?

- Can remote management be restricted to certain firewall interfaces and source IP addresses, such as those on a particular internal network?

- Does the firewall support centralized management for multiple devices (not necessarily just firewalls) from the same vendor?

- If centralized management is available, is it performed by a vendor-specific application or can it be controlled by other applications?

■ Performance (generally for network firewalls only)

- What amount of throughput, maximum simultaneous connections, connections per second, and latency requirements must be met to prevent the firewall from being a bottleneck for network access, for both current and future traffic needs?

- Are load balancing and failover functionally required to ensure high availability?

- Is hardware-based vs. software-based firewall preference a consideration?

■ Integration

- Will the firewall require specific hardware to properly integrate within the organization's network infrastructure (specific power capabilities, specific type of network interface card [NIC], specific backup device, etc.)?

- Does the firewall need to be compatible with other devices on the network that provide security or other services?

- Does the firewall's logging interoperate with existing log management systems?

- Will installing a firewall require changes to other areas of the network?

■ Physical Environment (generally a consideration for network firewalls, although it may also apply to the centralized components of host-based firewall implementations)

- Where will the firewall be physically located to ensure physical security and protection from disasters?

- Is there adequate shelf or rack space at the physical location where the firewall will be placed?

- Will additional power, backup power, air conditioning, and/or network connections be required at the physical location?

■ Personnel

- Who will be responsible for managing the firewall?

- Will system administrators require training before the firewall is deployed?

■ Future Needs

- Will the firewall meet the future needs of the organization (plans to move to IPv6, anticipated bandwidth requirements, compliance with regulations expected to be implemented, etc.)?

Other items to consider when purchasing and implementing host-based and personal firewalls include:

■ Do workstations or servers meet the minimum system requirements of the firewall being evaluated?

■ Will the firewall be compatible with other security software on the workstation or server (e.g., antimalware software)?

■ Can the firewall be centrally managed and allow policies that enforce the organization's security policy to be pushed to clients?

■ Can the firewall report policy violations to a central server?

■ Can the firewall be locked down to prevent anyone but administrators from modifying its settings?

■ Will the firewall conflict with host-based or personal firewalls built in to the hosts' operating systems? If so, how easily can these conflicts be resolved?

5.2 Configure

The configuration phase involves all facets of configuring the firewall platform. This includes installing hardware and software, configuring policies, configuring logging and alerting, and integrating the firewall into the network architecture.

5.2.1 Hardware and Software Installation

Once the firewall has been chosen and acquired, the hardware, operating system, and underlying firewall software should be installed for a software-based firewall. Next, for both software-based and hardware-based firewalls, patches and vendor updates should be installed on the system. During this stage, the firewall should also be hardened to decrease the risk of vulnerabilities and protect the system against unauthorized access. Any console software needed for remote access should also be installed at this time.

During the installation and configuration, only the administrator doing that work should be able to manage the firewall. All other management services for the firewall, such as SNMP, should be disabled, and these services should be left disabled permanently unless needed. If the firewall supports having a separate administrator account for each person performing firewall administration duties, configure such accounts.

Network firewalls should be placed in a room that meets the product's recommended environmental requirements for temperature, humidity, space, power, etc. This room should also be physically secured to prevent unauthorized personnel from accessing the firewall.

Comparing the logs of multiple systems when analyzing problems is very important, so the internal clocks in each firewall should be consistent with those in all other systems used by the organization. The best way to do this is to have all systems synchronize with an authoritative time source.

5.2.2 Policy Configuration

Once hardware and software has been installed and secured, administrators can create the firewall's policies. Some firewalls implement policy through explicit rules; some firewalls require configuring firewall settings that then create internal rules; some firewalls create policies and rules automatically; and still others use a combination of these three types of configuration. The end result is a set of rules called a *ruleset* that describes how the firewall acts. Some vendors have restrictions or suggestions on the order of the rules in a ruleset. While it is common to think of a firewall's rules affecting traffic that appears on the internal or external interfaces, most firewalls also allow configuring policies that are not traffic-based, such as who can view or change the rules, or where external DNS servers and time synchronization servers can be found.

These rulesets should implement the organization's firewall policy as documented in the system security plan, and should be as specific as possible with regards to the network traffic they control. To create a ruleset, it should first be determined what types of traffic (protocols, source and destination addresses, etc.) are required by approved applications for the organization. This should include protocols that the firewall itself may need (DNS, Simple Network Management Protocol [SNMP], NTP, logging, etc.)

The details of creating a ruleset vary by type of firewall and specific products. For example, many firewalls check traffic against rules in a sequential manner until a match is found. For these firewalls, rules with the highest chance of matching traffic patterns should be placed as high in the list as possible to improve firewall performance. Other firewalls have more complex ways of processing rulesets, such as first checking "deny" rules and then checking "allow" rules.

Most firewalls allow each rule in a ruleset to have a comment. Filling in such a comment is important for others to determine why a rule was made. Comments are also quite useful to people auditing rulesets. Although commenting rules may seem trivial, it can be quite valuable later and takes little effort. The rule changes and the associated comments should be copied to the appropriate configuration management log.

At minimum, the following rules should be defined:

- Port filtering should be enabled at the outer edge of the network, and probably at places inside the network as well.

- Content filtering should be done as close to the content receiver as possible.

Many ways exist to define rules, and each organization will have its own needs and specific sets of personnel who should be involved in ruleset configuration.

If multiple firewalls need to have the same rules or a common subset of rules, those rules should be synchronized across the firewalls. This is usually done in a vendor-specific fashion. Note that it is likely that some of the firewalls might have somewhat different policies, depending on their location in the organization's network. For example, an organization might want to have just one of its firewalls acting as the VPN gateway, although all the firewalls might have the same filtering rules for non-VPN traffic. Therefore, it is important to only synchronize the rules that are common across the firewalls.

5.2.3 Logging and Alerts Configuration

The next step in the configuration process is to set up logging and alerts. Logging is a critical step in preventing and recovering from failures as well as ensuring that proper security configurations are set on the firewall. Proper logging can also provide vital information for responding to security incidents. Whenever possible, the firewall should be configured both to store logs locally and to send them to a centralized log management infrastructure. Resource constraints, firewall logging capabilities, and other situations may impair the ability to store logs both locally and centrally.

Deciding what to log, and how long to keep logs, should be done on a case-by-case basis. For example, some network administrators want to log all incoming accepted connections so that they can make sure that they are not accepting unwanted traffic. Other administrators would not want to log accepted incoming connections because they are so numerous or because the logging would consume too many resources. Similarly, some administrators would not want to log all incoming traffic denied by the firewall because the number of scans and probes by potentially malicious parties is very high and there is no action to be taken in response to them; however, other administrators would want to know about scans and probes in case they can detect a pattern that alerts them to a potential attack that can then be prevented.

If the firewall supports having administrator accounts with different capabilities, create one or more administrative user accounts with just read access to the logs, if possible. Use these credentials when performing read-only tasks such as auditing and periodic inspection of the logs.

In addition to configuring logging, real-time alerts should also be set up to notify administrators when important events occur on the firewall. Notifications may include the following:

- Any modifications or disabling of the firewall rules

- System reboots, disk shortages, and other operational events

■ Secondary system status changes, if applicable.

5.3 Test

New firewalls should be tested and evaluated before deployment to ensure that they are working properly. Testing should be completed on a test network without connectivity to the production network. This test network should attempt to replicate the production network as faithfully as possible, including the network topology and network traffic that would travel through the firewall. Aspects of the solution to evaluate include the following:

■ **Connectivity.** Users can establish and maintain connections through the firewall.

■ **Ruleset**, Traffic that is specifically allowed by the security policy is permitted. All traffic that is not allowed by the security policy is blocked. Verification of the ruleset should include both reviewing it manually and testing whether the rules work as expected.

■ **Application Compatibility.** Host-based or personal firewall solutions do not break or interfere with the use of existing software applications. This includes network communications between application components. Network firewall solutions do not interfere with applications that have components that interact through the firewall (e.g., client and server software).

■ **Management.** Administrators can configure and manage the solution effectively and securely.

■ **Logging.** Logging and data management function in accordance with the organization's policies and strategies.

■ **Performance.** Solutions provide adequate performance during normal and peak usage. In many cases, the best way to test performance under the load of a prototype implementation is to use simulated traffic generators on a live test network to mimic the actual characteristics of expected traffic as closely as possible. Simulating the loads caused by DoS attacks can also be helpful in assessing firewall performance. Testing should incorporate a variety of applications that will traverse the firewall, especially those that are most likely to be affected by network throughput or latency issues.

■ **Security of the Implementation.** The firewall implementation itself may contain vulnerabilities and weaknesses that attackers could exploit. Organizations with high security needs may want to perform vulnerability assessments against firewall components.

■ **Component Interoperability.** Components of the firewall solution must function together properly. This is of greatest concern when a variety of components from different vendors are used.

■ **Policy Synchronization.** If there are multiple firewalls running synchronized policies or groups of rules, test that the synchronization works in various scenarios (such as if one or more nodes are offline).

■ **Additional Features.** Additional features that will be used by the firewall—such as VPN and antimalware capabilities—should be tested to ensure they are working properly.

5.4 Deploy

Once testing is complete and all issues have been resolved, the next phase of the firewall planning and implementation model is deployment, which should be done in accordance with organization policies. Before deploying the firewall, administrators should notify users or owners of potentially affected systems of the planned deployment, and instruct them who to notify if they encounter any problems. Any changes required to other equipment should also be coordinated as part of the firewall deployment. The security policy expressed by the firewall's configuration should be added to the overall security policy of the organization, and the ongoing changes to its configuration should be integrated with the organization's configuration management processes. If multiple firewalls are being deployed, including personal firewalls or at multiple branch offices, a gradual or phased approach should be considered; a pilot program would also be helpful, especially for identifying and resolving issues of conflicting policies. This will provide administrators with an opportunity to evaluate the firewall solution's impact and resolve issues before enterprise-wide deployment.

Connecting a firewall to the organization's network requires more than just inserting the firewall into the traffic flow from the outside of the network to the inside: it also involves integrating the firewall with other network elements that will interact with the firewall. Because firewalls usually act as routers, the firewall has to be integrated into the network's routing structure. This often means replacing a router that is at the same spot in the network topology as where the firewall is being placed, but it can also mean changing the routing tables for other routers in the organization's network to handle the addition of this new router. If elements in the network use dynamic routing, those elements will probably need to have their configuration modified to be aware of the firewall's routing. Also, the network switch on the outside of the network being protected may need to be reconfigured to handle the firewall's addressing. If the firewall is a set of systems with failover between the systems, the network switch may need to be configured to handle the failover.

5.5 Manage

This last phase of the firewall planning and implementation model is the longest lasting, because managing the solution involves maintaining firewall architecture, policies, software, and other components of the solution chosen to be deployed. One example of a typical maintenance action is testing and applying patches to firewall devices.[21] Policy rules may need to be updated as new threats are identified and requirements change, such as when new applications or hosts are implemented within the network, and should also be reviewed periodically to ensure they remain in compliance with security policy. It is also important to monitor the performance of firewall components to ensure that potential resource issues are identified and addressed before components become overwhelmed. Logs and alerts should also be monitored continuously to identify threats—successful and unsuccessful—that are made to the system. Another important task is to perform periodic testing to verify that firewall rules are functioning as expected. Also, firewall policies and rulesets should be backed up regularly. Some firewalls can store this information in multiple formats, such as a binary format that is used to configure the firewall and a human-readable format that can be read by auditors. If multiple formats are available, backups should be kept in all of them.

Changes to firewall rulesets or policies impact security and should be managed as part of a formal configuration management process. Many firewalls have auditing of changes as part of their administrative interfaces, but this does not necessarily track policy changes. At a minimum, a log should be kept of all policy decisions and ruleset changes—and this log should somehow be associated with the firewall. For example, the log can be attached to the device physically, or the log file can be kept in the same part of the organization's inventory management system as the firewall. Also, some firewalls permit comments to be maintained for each rule; wherever practical, rulesets should be documented with comments on each rule. Most firewalls allow restrictions on who can make changes to the ruleset; some even allow restrictions on the addresses from which administrators can make such changes. Such restrictions should be used when possible.

---

[21] For additional information about patch management, see NIST SP 800-40 Version 2, *Creating a Patch and Vulnerability Management Program* (http://csrc.nist.gov/publications/PubsSPs.html).

Be aware that firewall rulesets can become increasingly complicated with age. For example, a new firewall ruleset might contain entries to accommodate only outbound user traffic and inbound email traffic (along with allowing the return inbound connections required by TCP/IP)—but will likely contain far more rules by the time the firewall system reaches the end of its first year in production. While new user or business requirements typically drive these changes, they can also reflect other influences within an organization. It is important to review the firewall policy often. Such a review can uncover rules that are no longer needed as well as new policy requirements that need to be added to the firewall.

It is best to review the firewall policy at regular intervals so that such reviews do not only happen during policy or security audits (or, worse, only during emergencies). Each review should include a detailed examination of all changes since the last regular review, particularly who made the changes and under what circumstances. It is also useful to occasionally perform overall ruleset audits by people who are not part of the normal policy review team to get an outside view of how the policy matches the organization's goals. Some firewalls have tools that can do automated reviews of policies, looking for such things as redundant rules or missing rules that are widely recommended. If such tools are available for an organization's firewall, they should be used periodically, probably as part of the regular policy review.

Organizations may want to consider conducting penetration testing to assess the overall security of their network environment. This testing can be used to verify that a firewall ruleset is performing as intended by generating network traffic and monitoring how it is handled by the firewall in comparison with its expected response. Penetration testing should be employed in addition to, rather than instead of, a conventional audit program.[22]

---

[22] For more information on penetration testing, see NIST SP 800-115, *Technical Guide to Information Security Testing and Assessment* (http://csrc.nist.gov/publications/PubsSPs.html).

Appendix A—Glossary

Selected terms used in the publication are defined below.

Application Firewall: A firewall that uses stateful protocol analysis to analyze network traffic for one or more applications.

Application-Proxy Gateway: A firewall capability that combines lower-layer access control with upper layer-functionality, and includes a proxy agent that acts as an intermediary between two hosts that wish to communicate with each other.

Dedicated Proxy Server: A form of proxy server that has much more limited firewalling capabilities than an application-proxy gateway.

Demilitarized Zone (DMZ): An interface on a routing firewall that is similar to the interfaces found on the firewall's protected side. Traffic moving between the DMZ and other interfaces on the protected side of the firewall still goes through the firewall and can have firewall protection policies applied.

Deny by Default: To block all inbound and outbound traffic that has not been expressly permitted by firewall policy.

Egress Filtering: Filtering of outgoing network traffic.

Firewall: A device or program that controls the flow of network traffic between networks or hosts that employ differing security postures.

Host-Based Firewall: A software-based firewall installed on a server to monitor and control its incoming and outgoing network traffic.

Ingress Filtering: Filtering of incoming network traffic.

Network Access Control (NAC): A feature provided by some firewalls that allows access based on a user's credentials and the results of health checks performed on the telework client device.

Network Address Translation (NAT): A routing technology used by many firewalls to hide internal system addresses from an external network through use of an addressing schema.

Packet Filter: A routing device that provides access control functionality for host addresses and communication sessions.

Personal Firewall: A software-based firewall installed on a desktop or laptop computer to monitor and control its incoming and outgoing network traffic.

Personal Firewall Appliance: A device that performs functions similar to a personal firewall for a group of computers on a home network.

Ruleset: A set of directives that govern the access control functionality of a firewall. The firewall uses these directives to determine how packets should be routed between its interfaces.

Stateful Inspection: Packet filtering that also tracks the state of connections and blocks packets that deviate from the expected state.

Stateful Protocol Analysis: A firewalling capability that improves upon standard stateful inspection by adding basic intrusion detection technology. This technology consists of an inspection engine that analyzes protocols at the application layer to compare vendor-developed profiles of benign protocol activity against observed events to identify deviations, allowing a firewall to allow or deny access based on how an application is running over a network.

Stateless Inspection: See "Packet Filtering".

Appendix B—Acronyms and Abbreviations

Selected acronyms and abbreviations used in the publication are defined below.

AH	Authentication Header
ALG	Application Layer Gateways
CA	Certificate Authority
CIDR	Classless Inter-Domain Routing
CPU	Central Processing Unit
DMZ	Demilitarized Zone
DNS	Domain Name System
DoS	Denial of Service
ESP	Encapsulating Security Payload
FISMA	Federal Information Security Management Act
FTP	File Transfer Protocol
HA	High Availability
HTML	Hypertext Markup Language
HTTP	Hypertext Transfer Protocol
ICMP	Internet Control Message Protocol
IDPS	Intrusion Detection and Prevention System
IETF	Internet Engineering Task Force
IGMP	Internet Group Management Protocol
IKE	Internet Key Exchange
IM	Instant Messaging
IMAP	Internet Message Access Protocol
IP	Internet Protocol
IPS	Intrusion Prevention System
IPsec	Internet Protocol Security
IPv4	Internet Protocol version 4
IPv6	Internet Protocol version 6
ISATAP	Intra-site Automatic Tunnel Addressing Protocol
ISP	Internet Service Provider
IT	Information Technology
ITL	Information Technology Laboratory
LAN	Local Area Network
LDAP	Lightweight Directory Access Protocol
MAC	Media Access Control
MIME	Multipurpose Internet Mail Extensions
NAC	Network Access Control
NAP	Network Access Protection
NAPT	Network Address and Port Translation
NAT	Network Address Translation

NIC	Network Interface Card
NIST	National Institute of Standards and Technology
NTP	Network Time Protocol
OMB	Office of Management and Budget
PAT	Port Address Translation
PC	Personal Computer
PCI	Payment Card Industry
PMTU	Path Maximum Transmission Unit
POP	Post Office Protocol
RADIUS	Remote Authentication Dial In User Service
RFC	Request for Comments
SMTP	Simple Mail Transfer Protocol
SNMP	Simple Network Management Protocol
SP	Special Publication
SQL	Structured Query Language
SSL	Secure Sockets Layer
TCP	Transmission Control Protocol
TCP/IP	Transmission Control Protocol/Internet Protocol
TLS	Transport Layer Security
UDP	User Datagram Protocol
UPnP	Universal Plug and Play
URL	Uniform Resource Locator
UTM	Unified Threat Management
VoIP	Voice over Internet Protocol
VPN	Virtual Private Network
VPNC	Virtual Private Network Consortium
WAN	Wide Area Network
XML	Extensible Markup Language

Appendix C—Resources

The lists below provide examples of resources that may be helpful.

NIST Documents and Resource Sites

Resource Name	Uniform Resource Locator (URL)
NIST National Checklist Program	http://checklists.nist.gov/
NIST SP 800-18 Revision 1, *Guide for Developing Security Plans for Federal Information Systems*	http://csrc.nist.gov/publications/nistpubs/800-18-Rev1/sp800-18-Rev1-final.pdf
NIST SP 800-30, *Risk Management Guide for Information Technology Systems*	http://csrc.nist.gov/publications/nistpubs/800-30/sp800-30.pdf
NIST SP 800-40 Version 2, *Creating a Patch and Vulnerability Management Program*	http://csrc.nist.gov/publications/nistpubs/800-40-Ver2/SP800-40v2.pdf
NIST SP 800-44 Version 2, *Guidelines on Securing Public Web Servers*	http://csrc.nist.gov/publications/nistpubs/800-44-ver2/SP800-44v2.pdf
NIST SP 800-45 Version 2, *Guidelines on Electronic Mail Security*	http://csrc.nist.gov/publications/nistpubs/800-45-version2/SP800-45v2.pdf
NIST SP 800-46 Revision 1, *Guide to Enterprise Telework and Remote Access Security*	http://csrc.nist.gov/publications/nistpubs/800-46-rev1/sp800-46r1.pdf
NIST SP 800-52, *Guidelines for the Selection and Use of Transport Layer Security (TLS) Implementations*	http://csrc.nist.gov/publications/nistpubs/800-52/SP800-52.pdf
NIST SP 800-61 Revision 1, *Computer Security Incident Handling Guide*	http://csrc.nist.gov/publications/nistpubs/800-61-rev1/SP800-61rev1.pdf
NIST SP 800-70 Revision 1 (Draft), *National Checklist Program for IT Products—Guidelines for Checklist Users and Developers*	http://csrc.nist.gov/publications/PubsSPs.html
NIST SP 800-77, *Guide to IPsec VPNs*	http://csrc.nist.gov/publications/nistpubs/800-77/sp800-77.pdf
NIST SP 800-81 Revision 1 (Draft), *Secure Domain Name System (DNS) Deployment Guide*	http://csrc.nist.gov/publications/PubsSPs.html
NIST SP 800-86, *Guide to Integrating Forensic Techniques into Incident Response*	http://csrc.nist.gov/publications/nistpubs/800-86/SP800-86.pdf
NIST SP 800-92, *Guide to Computer Security Log Management*	http://csrc.nist.gov/publications/nistpubs/800-92/SP800-92.pdf
NIST SP 800-94, *Guide to Intrusion Detection and Prevention Systems (IDPS)*	http://csrc.nist.gov/publications/nistpubs/800-94/SP800-94.pdf
NIST SP 800-95, *Guide to Secure Web Services*	http://csrc.nist.gov/publications/nistpubs/800-95/SP800-95.pdf
NIST SP 800-97, *Establishing Wireless Robust Security Networks: A Guide to IEEE 802.11i*	http://csrc.nist.gov/publications/nistpubs/800-97/SP800-97.pdf
NIST SP 800-113, *Guide to SSL VPNs*	http://csrc.nist.gov/publications/nistpubs/800-113/SP800-113.pdf
NIST SP 800-114, *User's Guide to Securing External Devices for Telework and Remote Access*	http://csrc.nist.gov/publications/nistpubs/800-114/SP800-114.pdf
NIST SP 800-115, *Technical Guide to Information Security Testing and Assessment*	http://csrc.nist.gov/publications/nistpubs/800-115/SP800-115.pdf

Other Technical Resource Sites and Documents

Resource Name	Uniform Resource Locator (URL)
Achieving Defense-in-Depth with Internal Firewalls	http://www.sans.org/reading_room/whitepapers/firewalls/797.php?portal=a4d358dbd051422110d917753a0ebb7c
Best Practices for Managing Firewall Logs	http://www.zdnet.com.au/insight/print.htm?TYPE=story&AT=120265680-139023731t-110000100c
Defense in Depth: Foundations for Secure and Resilient IT Enterprises	http://www.cert.org/archive/pdf/Defense_in_Depth092106.pdf
Firewall Evolution – Deep Packet Inspection	http://www.securityfocus.com/infocus/1716
How do Circuit-Level Gateways and Application-Level Gateways Differ?	http://searchsecurity.techtarget.com/expert/KnowledgebaseAnswer/0,289625,sid14_gci1197999,00.html
National Vulnerability Database	http://nvd.nist.gov/
The Perils of Deep Packet Inspection	http://www.securityfocus.com/infocus/1817
Transparent, Bridging Firewall Devices	http://www.securityfocus.com/infocus/1737
The Web Services Advisor: XML Firewalls	http://searchwebservices.techtarget.com/tip/1,289483,sid26_gci855052,00.html